B   SACAGAWEA
Blassingame, Wyatt
Sacagawea: Indian guide Copy 1

SACAGAWEA
INDIAN GUIDE

BY WYATT BLASSINGAME

ILLUSTRATED BY EDWARD SHENTON

GARRARD PUBLISHING COMPANY

CHAMPAIGN, ILLINOIS

To Tani

My small periwinkle picking friend

ALICE MARRIOTT and CAROL K. RACHLIN of Southwest Research Associates are consultants for Garrard Indian Books.

MISS MARRIOTT has lived among the Kiowa and Cheyenne Indians in Oklahoma and spent many years with the Pueblos of New Mexico and the Hopis of Arizona. First woman to take a degree in anthropology from the University of Oklahoma, she is a Fellow of the American Anthropological Association, now working with its Curriculum Project.

MISS RACHLIN, also a Fellow of AAA and of the American Association for the Advancement of Science, is a graduate in anthropology of Columbia University. She has done archaeological work in New Jersey and Indiana, and ethnological field work with Algonquian tribes of the Midwest.

Manufactured in the United States of America
Library of Congress Catalog Card Number: 65-17170

Contents

The Shoshones

Sacagawea's people, the Northern Shoshones Indians of the Rockies, were part of a larger family of Shoshones. They lived in the Great Basin, a large dry area including parts of California, Nevada, Utah, Idaho and Wyoming.

Since most of this area was desert and not good for farming or hunting, the Shoshones had trouble finding food. During the summer, small groups roamed the Great Basin looking for seeds, pine nuts, roots and grasshoppers. In the winter, they settled in small villages.

Because they were poor, the Shoshones could not afford good houses or food for many people at tribal ceremonies. So once a year, they gathered for a rabbit or antelope hunt. After the hunt, the people joined in singing and dancing.

The mountain Shoshones, Sacagawea's people, began to use horses. They lived in tepees and danced the Sun Dance like the wealthier Plains Indians. These were the Shoshones from whom Lewis and Clark bought horses to cross the mountains.

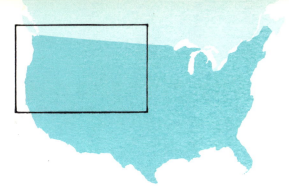

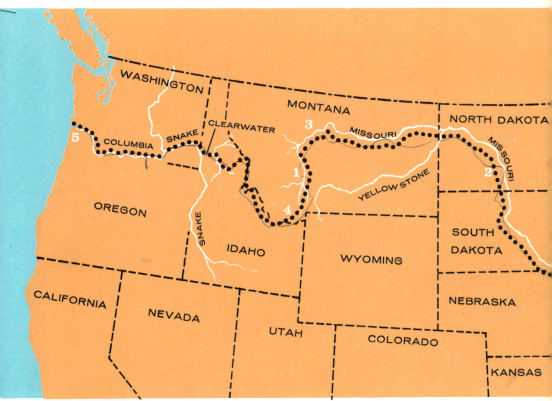

●●●●●●● The route of Lewis and Clark

1. Sacagawea was stolen from her tribe in this area.

2. The Mandan village, where Sacagawea met Lewis and Clark.

3. The Great Falls, where Sacagawea nearly died from her illness.

4. Lewis and Clark bought horses from the Shoshones here.

5. Fort Clatsop, where Sacagawea celebrated Christmas and went to see the whale.

1

Captured!

The girl ate the buffalo meat raw. There was no time to cook it. She was too hungry. She held the raw meat in her hands and tore at it with her teeth. All the other Indians, standing around the dead buffalo, ate in the same way.

The girl's name was Sacagawea. She did not know how old she was—twelve or thirteen summers. Her people, the Shoshones, kept no record of time. Time did not matter. What mattered was food. It seemed to Sacagawea that all her life she had been hungry.

Sacagawea's people were a small tribe. In the summers they lived high in the Rocky Mountains. They ate berries and fish and wild game. There was rarely enough. But they were safe here from their enemies, the Minnetarees and other powerful tribes who lived on the plains. In the fall, however, the berries were gone. The fish disappeared. The game went down from the mountains to the warmer valleys. The Shoshones had to follow the game or die of hunger.

On the plains they were often attacked by other tribes. The Shoshone warriors were brave, but they did not have guns like the Minnetaree braves. Guns came from white men. In 1800 white men had never visited the country of the Shoshones.

This autumn the Shoshones had made camp on the bank of a small river. The hunters rode out to look for buffalo. They killed one near camp, then rode away after others. The women and children and old men ran to the dead buffalo. Hurriedly, they skinned the animal where it lay. They sliced the raw meat and began to eat it. They were too excited to think about danger.

Suddenly, someone screamed. Looking up, Sacagawea saw Indians riding fast over the hill. She saw the naked and painted bodies, heard the wild war whoops. She knew at once they were Minnetarees.

Sacagawea ran. She was a small, skinny girl with long, straight black hair. But she ran like a deer. Even so, the Minnetaree warriors reached the camp ahead of her. They captured the Shoshone horses.

Sacagawea turned toward the river. She dived in and swam to where willow trees hung over the bank. Behind her she heard the shouts of the warriors. She heard loud, banging noises that she knew must be guns.

The willows gave a little protection, but not much. Slowly Sacagawea began to creep upstream.

She came to a place where there were
no willows to hide her. Should she try
to cross the open space?

Sacagawea looked back. Two Indians
were riding their horses up the middle
of the stream. One of them saw her
and shouted. The horses rushed forward.

Sacagawea tried to run to the bank.
She heard the horse splashing behind

her. She expected to feel a knife in her
back. Instead, something caught her by
the arm. She was lifted like a doll and
flung across the back of the horse.

Sacagawea fought to get free, but the
man held her easily. He was a huge
man, almost a giant. His face was
smeared with war paint and he had
only one eye.

2

Slave of the Minnetarees

The Minnetaree warriors rode away before the Shoshone braves could return from their hunt. They took with them the women and children they had captured. Sacagawea was one of these. She was not hurt, but there was no chance to escape.

Sacagawea knew that she would be a slave in the land of the Minnetarees.

She would belong to the one-eyed giant who had captured her. She would have to work hard. But she was used to work. And on the plains there were many buffalo. Perhaps she would have plenty to eat. Perhaps life would not be too bad after all, even though she would miss her family.

After many day's travel, they reached the Minnetaree village. The houses here were not like any Sacagawea had ever seen. Her people lived in tepees made of brush. The Minnetaree houses were made of dirt. They were round and dome-shaped, with a door in the side. In the middle of each house was a place for a fire. There was a hole in the roof for the smoke to escape. Such a house would be warm even in winter.

The one-eyed giant who had captured Sacagawea had many wives, as was the custom with these Indians. He gave Sacagawea to his wives and told them to put her to work. The work was much the same as she had done at home. There were buffalo hides to scrape and make into robes. The skins of deer and antelope were made into moccasins. One job, however, was new to Sacagawea. Her own people ate the berries and plants that grew wild, but they had no farms. The Minnetarees raised their own corn and squash. When spring came, one of Sacagawea's jobs was to dig the ground for a garden. She used a hoe made from the shoulder bone of a buffalo. When the ground was ready, she learned to plant the seed.

It did not occur to Sacagawea that this was work for a man. Among the Indians most work in the fields was done by the women. Sacagawea did not mind. If she worked, there would be more food to eat.

Little by little, Sacagawea learned the language of the Minnetarees. Also she learned the sign language used by all the Indians of the plains. The two forefingers put together, pointing up, meant a tepee. The same fingers held beside the head like horns meant buffalo. The first two fingers of one hand placed across the other wrist meant a man on horseback. Sacagawea knew some of these signs already because her people used them. But they did not use signs as much as the plains Indians.

Several years passed. Sacagawea was still small, but she was strong. She was growing into womanhood.

Each winter two or three white men visited the village of the Minnetarees. These were trappers and hunters. They lived with the Indians when the streams were frozen and there was no place to set their beaver traps. Some of them were French Canadians. Some were men from the United States east of the Mississippi River. Sacagawea did not know where these countries were. When she heard the white men talk together she could not understand anything they said.

One of the white men was a French trapper named Toussaint Charbonneau. He had a thick black beard and a loud voice. Sometimes he visited the one-eyed giant who had captured Sacagawea. He noticed the pretty little Shoshone slave sitting quietly in the back of the lodge. He saw how she listened when he talked. He was much older than Sacagawea, but her looks and attention pleased him.

One day the giant called Sacagawea. "The white man, Charbonneau, has bought you for his wife," he said.

Sacagawea had known that one day she might be sold. Even if she had been still at home, her father might have sold her in the same way. It was the Indian custom. Life might be exciting as the wife of a white man, Sacagawea thought. But she said nothing.

"Charbonneau will come for you soon," the giant said. "Be ready to go with him."

Sacagawea had no choice. She nodded yes.

3

Hired by
Lewis and Clark

For Sacagawea, life with Charbonneau was not much different from life with the Minnetarees. He had several Indian wives. She helped them cook his food and make his clothes. She helped skin the animals he trapped.

One winter when she was sixteen or seventeen years old they stayed with

some Mandan Indians. Their village was on the Missouri River, near where the city of Bismarck, North Dakota, is today. A number of white men were staying here.

These strange men were explorers, Charbonneau told Sacagawea. They were soldiers from the United States, the land to the east. They planned to map the American west.

"The men are spending the winter here," Charbonneau said. "In the spring they will start west again. They will go on up the Missouri River. Then they will cross the Rocky Mountains and head for a big water called the Pacific Ocean. If they reach it, they will be the first white men ever to make this trip.

"Perhaps I can get a job with them," Charbonneau went on. "They will need someone who knows how to talk to the Indians along the way."

Sacagawea's eyes were bright. "If they follow this river into the mountains, they will go to my home country. Oh! I would love to go with them!"

Charbonneau laughed. "You are a woman. You are about to have a baby. How could you make such a long, dangerous trip?"

"My baby will be born before spring. I could take it with me."

"You are foolish," Charbonneau said. "These men do not want a woman on their journey."

He left her and went to see the American soldiers. But soon he was

back. He was angry. "Come on," he told Sacagawea. "The American officers want to see you."

Quietly she followed Charbonneau to the hut where the American officers lived.

Captain Meriwether Lewis was a slim, dark, serious-looking man. The other officer, Captain William Clark, had red hair and blue eyes that twinkled as if he were about to laugh. They asked Charbonneau questions, and he in turn asked Sacagawea.

"Is she a Shoshone Indian?"

"Yes."

"Where do her people live?"

"In the mountains, near the headwaters of this river."

"Do they have horses?"

"Yes, they often have many horses."

"Are any members of her family still alive?"

Sacagawea's face became sad. She did not know. Perhaps they had all been killed by the Minnetarees.

"Does she still remember the Shoshone language?"

Sacagawea's face brightened. Of course she remembered.

The American captains looked at one another. "When we reach the head of this river," Captain Lewis said, "we must get horses to carry our supplies over the mountains. And we will have to get those horses from the Shoshones."

"If we take the girl with us," Captain Clark said, "she can help us get the horses from her people. I think we should hire Charbonneau—but only if he will take his wife."

Sacagawea could not understand these words, but Charbonneau did. He was angry because his wife seemed more important to these men than he did. But he did not let Sacagawea know this. "We have decided to let you go with us," he told her.

4

Little Pomp

Sacagawea's baby boy was born in February. Charbonneau gave him the French name Baptiste. But Sacagawea called her baby Pomp. In her language this meant "firstborn."

All the American soldiers took an interest in the young mother and her baby. They came to Charbonneau's earth lodge to visit. They would chuck the baby under the chin and laugh.

"Little Pomp," they called him. Captain Clark brought Sacagawea a present. It was a belt of blue beads. Sacagawea thought it was the prettiest thing she had ever seen, except her baby.

Both Captain Lewis and Captain Clark had studied some medicine before starting their journey. Now they did everything they could to help Sacagawea and Little Pomp grow strong and well.

Yet they wondered if the young mother would be able to carry her baby all the way to the mountains. "She's not much bigger than a child herself," Captain Clark said.

At last the day came to start up the river. The party went in eight small boats. Sometimes the men rowed.

Sometimes they used sails. Sometimes Sacagawea carried Little Pomp in her lap. But most of the time she carried him in a cradle strapped on her back. He laughed and gurgled. "I think," Captain Clark said, "that Little Pomp believes this whole trip is just to keep him happy."

When the boats stopped for the night, Sacagawea went walking along the riverbank. She carried a sharp pointed stick. Now and then she stuck it in the ground near a pile of driftwood. "What is she doing?" Captain Lewis asked Charbonneau.

"She is looking for food."

"Food?" the Captain asked. "What kind of food?"

Charbonneau explained that mice would sometimes gather wild artichokes and bury them. Sacagawea had learned from her people how to find these hiding places. Sure enough, the Indian girl soon returned to camp. Her skirts were filled with wild artichokes. She also had roots of other kinds that the Indians ate. Now the soldiers ate them too.

"These are good," one of the soldiers said.

"I thought it was a mistake to bring the Indian girl on this journey," another said, eating hungrily. "Now I am glad to have her. She is as good at getting food as our best hunter."

Another time there was even more reason to be glad Sacagawea was with them. Camping for the night, they found the ashes of an Indian fire. Around it were many tracks. Lewis and Clark were worried. Suppose these Indians were on the warpath?

Sacagawea saw the tracks. She bent down to study them carefully. From the way the moccasins were made, she knew what tribe these Indians belonged to. "These are friendly Indians," she told Charbonneau, who told Captain Lewis.

Lewis sighed with relief. "This little girl is more help than we expected," he told Captain Clark.

5

Boat Overturned!

It was early spring. High in the mountains the snow was just melting. The icy water flowed into the Missouri and flooded the great river. It made it difficult for the boats to fight their way upstream. But day after day the men kept on.

One day the wind blew harder than usual. There were big waves on the river. Sacagawea, with Little Pomp on her back, was in the largest boat. This was a big canoe with a sail, called the white pirogue. Charbonneau was steering. He could not swim and was afraid of the water. There were also two other men in the boat who could not swim. Cruzatte, a skilled boatman, was in the bow.

The boat held many valuable supplies, as Captain Lewis wrote later. *"Our papers, instruments, books, medicine, a great part of our merchandise, and in short almost every article . . . necessary to . . . insure the success of the enterprise."*

Suddenly a great gust of wind hit the

pirogue broadside. It made the boat lean far over. Frightened, Charbonneau steered in the wrong direction. The pirogue rolled almost on its side. The passengers did not fall out, but water began to pour into the boat. Terrified, Charbonneau began to jump crazily about. In another moment he would turn the boat over completely. Everyone and everything in it would be lost.

Both Lewis and Clark were on the riverbank at this time. They saw what was happening. They began to shout orders, but the boat was too far away for them to be heard. They thought about jumping into the river and swimming to help. But they knew the current was too strong. They would be swept downstream and drowned.

"If the boat goes all the way over," Clark muttered, "three men will drown. We will lose our most valuable supplies. We will have to turn back."

Then, to their amazement, they saw what was happening. In spite of the danger, Sacagawea was behaving with perfect calm. As the water poured into the boat, many of the supplies began to float. But before they could float away, the girl quickly gathered them up.

At the same time Cruzatte was ordering Charbonneau to be still. Then Cruzatte cut the sail away. With its weight gone, Cruzatte got the boat right side up. It was almost full of water, but the men managed to row it ashore. Sacagawea held the supplies safe in her arms.

Captain Clark began to laugh. "And we worried about bringing her," he said. "She certainly saved us this time."

Farther on they passed a river that flowed into the Missouri. They named it the Sacagawea in honor of her courage. The little Indian girl was very proud.

Later they came to a place where the Missouri branched into two streams. These were almost the same size. Lewis and Clark knew that one of them would lead high into the Rocky Mountains. This was the one they wanted to follow. But which one was it?

"There are great falls on the river that flows from the mountains," Sacagawea said. "I have never seen them, but I have heard my people talk about them."

Lewis and Clark decided the south
branch of the river might be the right
one. To make sure, Captain Lewis went
ahead to search for the falls. Captain
Clark followed with the boats.

That night Sacagawea felt sudden, terrible pains in her stomach. She tried not to cry, but Charbonneau heard her moan. He ran for Captain Clark.

The medicine Clark gave Sacagawea helped only a little. She was very sick. Yet the party had to keep going ahead.

The river now ran between steep walls. It was so swift the boats could not be rowed. The men had to wade in the water and pull them along with ropes. Icy water kept splashing into the boats, yet Sacagawea was too sick to walk. Day after day she lay huddled in the pirogue.

Captain Clark did everything he could to make her well. But he was a soldier, not a real doctor. He did not know what was wrong with Sacagawea. He was afraid she was going to die.

6

Flash Flood

Sacagawea lay in the boat with a high fever. Sometimes she could not think clearly. She dreamed she was a little girl eating buffalo. Then the buffalo changed into a one-eyed giant riding up to capture her. Another time she dreamed that she and Little Pomp were in the strange world of white men. They walked along paved streets between houses big as mountains.

Then her mind would be clear again and she would know she was in the pirogue. She could hear the water rushing past. Little Pomp would be lying beside her.

Finally the fever was gone. There were no more strange dreams. Captain Clark was happy when he brought her medicine. "You are going to get well."

While Sacagawea was sick, Captain Lewis had gone ahead and found the great falls. He knew now the party was on the right river. He came back and told Captain Clark to hurry.

As they got closer, Sacagawea could hear the falls. They made a great roaring noise, like thunder. "We'll have to find a way to get our boats around them," Captain Lewis said.

The boats were too heavy to carry on such a long march. The men cut down trees. They made wheels from the tree trunks. They made rude wagons to fit on the wheels. They put the boats and supplies on the wagons. With some men pushing and some pulling, they took the wagons to the other side of the falls. Then they came back for another load.

It took several weeks to get all the supplies past the falls. During this time Sacagawea stayed in camp. She was still weak, but getting stronger.

Finally Captain Clark asked if she was strong enough to walk. "I am strong," she told him. She was proud she could say the words in English.

She carried Little Pomp in the cradle on her back. Captain Clark and Charbonneau were with her. In many places cactus grew thickly. Their sharp thorns cut through Sacagawea's moccasins. Sometimes there were deep canyons to cross. It was hard climbing their steep sides, but Sacagawea did not complain.

They were in a deep canyon when lightning began to flash. Thunder boomed. "We have got to find shelter in a hurry," Captain Clark said. He led the way to a big rock that hung from the canyon wall. Sacagawea took the cradle off her back and put it on the ground beside her.

Hail began to fall, but they were safe under the big rock. Then a cloudburst came. Water began to run in streams around their feet. Sacagawea took Little Pomp out of his cradle and held him.

"Listen!" Charbonneau said suddenly.

From up the canyon came a loud rumbling noise. Soon the water began to get deeper around their feet. Swiftly it climbed to their ankles, their knees. Looking up the canyon, Clark saw a great wall of water rushing toward them.

"Run!" Clark shouted. "Up the side of the canyon!"

Charbonneau ran, without waiting to help Sacagawea. She had Little Pomp in her arms. There was no time to get the cradle. Holding the baby in one arm, she clawed at the canyon wall with the other. Captain Clark stayed behind, pushing her ahead of him.

The flood of water rushed close below them. It carried away Pomp's cradle. But Sacagawea and her baby were safe.

7

Chief of the Shoshones

Sacagawea knew they were close to her home country now. She recognized the odd shape of a hill she had seen as a small child. She recognized an island in the river, then the place where the river forked into three branches. Soon they passed the exact spot where she had been captured by the Minnetarees.

Sacagawea was very excited, but she did not show it. She could not know what had happened to her people in the years she had been gone. She did not know if any of her family were still alive. She could only hope.

Now the river was climbing high into the mountains. Sacagawea had seen no Indians, but she knew they were nearby. She knew they were secretly watching the white soldiers. She saw the smoke from their fires, day after day.

Once more Captain Lewis went ahead with a small band of soldiers. On this trip he met a party of Shoshones. They spoke together in sign language. Lewis tried to tell the Shoshone chief that he and his men came as friends. He tried to explain that they wanted to buy horses.

Where, asked the chief, were the trade goods with which to pay for the horses?

Captain Lewis made signs to say they were coming up the river in boats.

The chief was not sure what Lewis had said. He was not sure these men were friends. But he and his people went with Lewis to meet the boats.

When Captain Clark arrived with the boats, he joined Captain Lewis in the chief's tent. This was to be a very important talk. The success of the whole journey would depend on getting horses from the Shoshones. Lewis and Clark sent for Sacagawea to interpret.

The little Indian came quietly into the tent. She knew women did not usually take part in such important talks. She sat shyly without looking at the men.

"Tell the chief," Captain Lewis said, "that we come as friends."

Sacagawea started to speak. For the first time she looked at the Shoshone chief. Her voice stopped. With a loud cry she jumped to her feet. She ran across the tent and threw her arms around the chief.

He was her brother, Cameahwait!

The chief was almost as happy to see Sacagawea as she was to see him. He listened gladly when she told him the white men came as friends. He promised to let them have all the horses they needed.

Once more Sacagawea had proved to be a great help to the expedition.

8

On to the Pacific

Sacagawea had a problem. It was one she had to solve by herself.

She had returned to her people. Now, would she stay here with them, or would she go with the white men to see the Great Water?

She thought about it carefully. Except for her brother and one nephew, all her family was dead. Charbonneau was her husband now. His job was to go with Lewis and Clark. She would go with him, she decided.

Ahead of them lay the most terrible part of the journey. They had to go through the very heart of the Rocky Mountains. At this height the air was thin and cold. It was hard to breathe. Often the trail was only a narrow path along the edge of a high cliff, or across the very top of a mountain. One wrong step by man or animal meant sudden death. In some places fallen trees lay thick across the trail, blocking the way. The men had to cut their path with axes.

It was September, but in the high mountains snow had begun to fall. All the game was gone. The men ate any berries they could find, and the roots Sacagawea dug. Once a starving wolf came close to the camp. The men killed and ate it.

Sacagawea remembered how her people had lived. They always had to leave the mountains in winter or starve. But these white men kept going west, deeper into the mountains.

Captain Clark hurt his hip and could hardly walk. Captain Lewis was sick. Most of the men were sick or hurt. All were weak from hunger. One day there was nothing to eat but a few candles. Silently Sacagawea ate the small piece given to her. She knew she

must save all the strength possible. She had to nurse Little Pomp.

At last the terrible trail began to go down hill. They came to a valley filled with green grass. They had crossed the Rocky Mountains!

Here was a river with many fish in it. Sacagawea and the men ate fish

until they were filled. Then the men
cut down trees and built boats. From
here they could float downstream.

All the way up the Missouri River
they had seen few Indians. Now they
passed village after village, first on the
Snake River, then on the Columbia.
Once more the soldiers were glad to

have Sacagawea with them. These western Indians never let women go with them to fight. When they saw Sacagawea they were sure the white men came in peace.

A long time the boats traveled down the Columbia River. One day Sacagawea heard a faint booming sound. It was like thunder, but different. The river got wider and wider, until it did not look like a river. Sacagawea put her hand in the water and tasted it. She spit it out. It was salty.

Suddenly all the men began to cheer. "We've made it! We've made it!"

Sacagawea wasn't sure if this was the ocean. But she cheered with the men as they turned the boats toward the shore.

9

Christmas, and a Whale

The men made camp in a forest on the south bank of the Columbia River. It was near where the city of Astoria, Oregon, stands today. From this camp Sacagawea could not see the Pacific. It was still several miles away. But the river was so wide that to her it looked almost like an ocean.

Lewis and Clark knew that white men had reached this place before them. These men had been Americans as well as English, Spanish and Russians. But they had all come by ship across the Pacific. The friendly Indians told Lewis and Clark that no white men had ever before come here by land.

It was almost winter now. There was no chance to recross the Rockies before spring. Heavy snows would block the trails. It would be too cold to travel. So the men set to work to build a fort in which to live. They named it Fort Clatsop, because the Indians who lived here called themselves Clatsops.

The men spent the winter getting ready for the trip back. Sacagawea helped them make new clothes and moccasins. The weather was bad. Sacagawea had never seen so much rain. Yet inside the fort it was cheerful enough.

Sacagawea heard the men talking about Christmas. She knew many of the white men's words, but she did not know Christmas. She asked Charbonneau what it meant.

Christmas, he said, was part of the white man's religion. On Christmas Day white men gave presents to their close friends.

Sacagawea thought about this. Of all the soldiers, Captain Clark was her favorite. He could not pronounce her name, so he called her Janey. He made jokes with her. He had saved her life in the flood. And when Little Pomp was born, he had given her the beautiful blue belt. What could she give to thank him?

One morning she heard the men shouting, "Merry Christmas!" She saw them giving little gifts to one another: a bit of saved tobacco, a handmade pipe. Lewis and Clark gave Sacagawea some beads. They had made toys for Little Pomp.

Shyly the Indian girl handed Captain Clark a bundle. In it were 24 white ermine tails. These were highly prized by the Indians as decorations for their clothing. Sacagawea had carried them, wrapped in her little bag of belongings,

all the way from Fort Mandan. It was the finest present of all that Christmas morning.

Not long after Christmas, Sacagawea heard the men talking about a whale. This was another word she did not know. Charbonneau told her it was a kind of fish, except it breathed air. And it was big—bigger than four or five buffalo put together. One had washed up on the shore of the ocean.

Sacagawea could not believe there was such an animal. "Take me to see it," she asked.

"It is too far," Charbonneau said.

"Well, I want to go," Sacagawea said. "And I want to see the ocean too."

Charbonneau refused, so Sacagawea asked Captain Clark.

"All right, Janey," Clark said, laughing. "Anybody who has come this far ought to be able to go a few miles farther."

It was a long walk in the rain, but that did not bother Sacagawea. She stood on the top of a low hill and

looked out over the ocean. She saw the great waves come rolling in to the beach. And she saw the whale.

She did not know which was the most wonderful, the ocean or the whale. But all her life she would remember both of them.

10

The Return

On March 23, 1806, the explorers got back in their canoes. They paddled away from Fort Clatsop, up the Columbia River. The long journey home had begun.

It was almost as difficult as the way out. They were often hungry. Sometimes they were without any food except for the roots Sacagawea found.

They passed through the land of the Shoshones, but this time they did not see any of Sacagawea's people. Finally they reached the Missouri River. From here it was easy to go downstream to the Mandan villages.

This was where Sacagawea and Charbonneau had joined the party. From here on Lewis and Clark would not need an interpreter. "But if you will come to St. Louis with us," Clark told Charbonneau, "I will make sure you get a job. When Little Pomp grows up, I will send him to school."

Charbonneau shook his head. "I have lived with the Indians too long. I wouldn't be happy in a city."

Clark turned to Sacagawea. "Janey," he said, "you know I love Little Pomp.

When he is older, bring him to me. I will do everything I can for him, just as if he were my son."

Sacagawa wanted her son to have the white man's knowledge. But she did not want him to leave her. "Maybe when he is older," she said.

Captain Clark got in the boat. The men began to paddle. Holding Little Pomp in her arms, Sacagawea waved good-by.

It was cold that winter in the Mandan village. There was little food. Charbonneau and his family were often hungry. In the spring Charbonneau went off trapping. He was back again in the late fall. "We are going to St. Louis," he said. "I don't want to stay here another winter."

Sacagawea was delighted. She remembered the dream she had when she was sick, of the white man's city. Now she would really see it. Also she would see her friend Captain Clark.

Clark gave Charbonneau a job as he promised. He gave him a house. It was only a log cabin, but it was the finest house Sacagawea had ever had.

Even so, she grew restless. She was

an Indian. In the city she felt closed in. Charbonneau too was restless. Before long he went back to trapping.

No one is sure what happened to Sacagawea after this. Perhaps she went with Charbonneau. One record says that the Indian wife of Charbonneau, age about 25, died of fever at a trapper's fort. But Charbonneau, like the Indians he lived with, often had more than one wife. The girl who died may not have been Sacagawea.

Some people believe Sacagawea stayed for several years in St. Louis. Then she went to live with Comanche Indians. They say she became the wife of a Comanche chief. When the chief died, Sacagawea returned to her own people. Here she lived to be a very old woman.

We do not know if this is true or not. But we are sure that Little Pomp stayed in St. Louis for several years. Captain Clark sent him to school. Later he met a German prince who was visiting America. The prince took Little Pomp back to Europe with him. Little Pomp was a man now, and called Baptiste. He lived with the prince and learned to speak many languages. But the Indian blood was strong in him. He returned to the West. There he became a trapper and a guide for explorers and soldiers. Then he went to live with his mother's people, the Shoshones.

If Sacagawea did return to her people, Baptiste would certainly have found her among them. It must have been a very happy reunion.